Moti
Reluctant Learners
at 14–16

Collins Tips for Busy Language Teachers are a collection of short, easy-to-read booklets which provide a mine of practical suggestions for modern language teaching. Bearing in mind that teachers are so busy, theory is kept to a minimum in favour of direct, easy-to-manage suggestions for classroom use and for students' individual learning. To facilitate the teacher's task, the emphasis is placed, as much as possible, on different ways of exploiting existing resources.

Martine Pillette is an author, educational consultant and distance-learning tutor. Martine has many years of experience as a teacher and as an assistant examiner for several examination groups.

Published by Collins Educational
An imprint of HarperCollinsPublishers Ltd
77-85 Fulham Palace Road
London W6 8JB

First published 1997, reprinted 1997

ISBN 0 00 320226 7

Martine Pillette asserts the moral right to be identified as the author of this work.

British Library Cataloguing in Publication Data
A catalogue record for this book is available from the British Library.

Edited by Victoria Millar
Design by Bob Vickers
Cover design by Bob Vickers
Commissioned illustrations by Peter Brown
Production by Delphina Kitson-Mills-Jones

Printed in Hong Kong

Introduction

When foreign language learning appears tantamount to climbing up a greasy pole, there are problems in store for students… and teachers. These are exacerbated when students with two to three years of language learning behind them feel they have achieved nothing.

The reasons for underachievement and poor motivation can be manifold:

- lack of confidence
- concern about the exam
- unclear about subject structure
- subject matter too hard/easy/babyish
- unstimulating subject matter
- lack of interest in the subject/the country
- having to 'speak foreign'
- lack of skills awareness
- specific learning difficulties

Suitable remedies too need to be explored from many angles, and different solutions work with different individuals. Is the student who claims to dislike foreigners truly biased against the country or merely demotivated by lack of progress in the language?

The practical tips contained in this booklet focus essentially on achieving lower GCSE grades but also include advice on getting nearer to middle grades. They seek to generate a more positive attitude – and therefore a greater degree of success – among students, by rethinking both content and skills.

Contents

I can't remember a thing! – making a fresh start

If students appear 'rusty' and less than keen, work on rebuilding self-confidence straightaway. Do not frighten them on day one with a detailed explanation of the exam format. First convince students of how much they *do* remember after all.

Suggestions

Use mime, objects, posters etc. for brainstorming to trigger memory, and praise students for what they remember.

Present a topic.

Im Klassenzimmer	**En la ciudad**	Les loisirs

Brainstorm for single words initially, then possibly move on to short sentences:

ein Buch
Hast du ein Buch?

Brainstorm on classroom language. Use a few students as guinea pigs, to demonstrate their understanding.

Elicit non-verbal responses to what you say from students. Base your examples as far as possible on the students' environment to make the language more real.

El señor Pérez es profesor de historia.

Il y a une patinoire à Raunds.

Talk about yourself to generate curiosity – and therefore concentration. Ask students to assess what you say and try to call your bluff, by guessing whether it is true or false. The guessing element removes the pressure while still demanding genuine concentration on the spoken word.

J'ai une voiture.

J'ai trois motos.

J'adore l'avion.

As a more advanced step, swap roles with students, having them talk and you guess.

List some topics as words on the board or numbered pictures. Ask students to categorise the words you say by naming the topic or saying the correct number.

Team competitions enhance motivation: which team can produce the most complete spider's web on a given topic? Keep a record of scores over a period of time. This has been known to improve attendance, especially among boys.

When approaching a task, students often think they are cheating or useless when in fact they are using the right skills for the job. They need reassuring. Present short, simple conversations on familiar topics.

Susi: Wann **beginnt** der **Film**?
Hans: Um neunzehn Uhr.
Susi: Und wann **endet** er?
Hans: Um einundzwanzig Uhr dreißig.

Vorsprung 1 Students' Book

Did they understand the key information? – praise them.
Did they use memory? Awareness of cognates? – praise them.
Did they make informed guesses based on visuals or context? – praise them.
Did they ignore the hard words that did not seem to matter? – praise them.

Why are we doing this? – short-term objectives

In spite of a topic-based approach, students often find it difficult to identify targets, or they lose track half-way through a topic. Nobody thrives on working in the dark. Students need to be given a clear sense of direction at all times.

Suggestions

Break each topic down into clear objectives and share these with the students.

Dans cette unité, vous allez réviser un peu et vous allez apprendre à:

1 vous préparer pour un entretien.

2 parler du travail que vous avez fait.

3 écrire un curriculum vitae.

4 parler de vous-même.

Vital 2 Students' Book

Relate any reference materials to these objectives to facilitate initial learning and revision later on.

Objectif 2 Parler du travail que vous avez fait

Vous avez déjà travaillé?	Have you worked before?
Oui, l'été dernier, j'ai travaillé dans un restaurant. C'était intéressant.	Yes, last summer I worked in a restaurant. It was interesting

Vital 2 Students' Book

At the end of a lesson or topic, always remind students of the new objectives achieved, or ask them to remind you!

When building upon a topic you have covered before, explain your reasons clearly to students. Otherwise they may think that they are just going to be doing the same old thing again. The new challenges need to be easy to identify.

Do we have to learn all this? – paring down the language

Excessively high expectations are an immediate turn off, especially when it comes to the quantity of language to be mastered. It is more realistic to focus on a more limited range and to work on quality instead.

Suggestions

There are many ways of asking the way to the post office.

Wo ist die Post?
Das weißt du nicht.
Du kannst fragen:

Die Post, bitte?

Wo ist die Post, bitte?

Wie komme ich zur Post, bitte?

You will have to understand all three questions in your exam, but you need use only one.
Choose the one which is easiest for you.

Vorsprung 1 Workbook

Show students you are on their side by teaching them the simplest phrase. Some of the others can be learnt by more able students, possibly for recognition purposes only.

Do the same with grammar. Ask yourself:

- what grammar areas do these students need to master?
- are those areas best taught through explicit grammatical explanations or as vocabulary items?

J'ai joué	au tennis au volley-ball au basket au ping-pong au football
J'ai visité	Paris des musées des châteaux
J'ai été	à la plage en discothèque dans des cafés au restaurant

Vital 1 Students' Book

Verbs:

- concentrate first and foremost on the first person singular.
- concentrate on key verbs only: how many verbs are really needed to describe last night/last week-end/last summer?

What does it mean anyway? – coping with new language

Problems arise when students try to use new language productively too soon. Sufficient time has to be devoted to recognition exercises, varying the type of response you expect so as to keep boredom at bay. This should be followed by carefully devised – and disguised – repetition and copying tasks, before more ambitious work takes place.

Suggestions

Recognition

Use categorising as a change from matching up.

> ***Positiv oder negativ?***
> ***Es ist eine saubere Stadt.***
> ***Es ist eine schmutzige Stadt.***

This approach is particularly useful when dealing with slightly more abstract language.

Also allow students to express their own opinions in their responses, thus moving away from the idea of a correct or incorrect answer. The suggestion here on opinions about towns can be used for reading or listening practice and lends itself to written, verbal or non-verbal responses.

> ***¿Estás de acuerdo, sí o no?***
> ***Rushden es una ciudad estupenda.***
> ***Es una ciudad divertida.***

Give students a purpose beyond merely understanding detailed information.

With this approach, students can reach a positive end result even though they may not understand every single piece of information.

Ecoutez la cassette. Voici une description.
C'est la description du chien ou de la femme?

Vital 1 Students' Book

Repetition

Opt for selective repetition.

Loisirs: répète seulement les sports.

Sprich nach:
a das ideale Haus für die Großeltern.
b das ideale Haus für eine Familie mit drei kleinen Kindern.

Vorsprung 1 Students' Book

This approach has two advantages:

- it is more 'grown-up' than blanket repetition
- it forces students to concentrate on the meaning of what they hear.

Once again, give students the opportunity of responding with an expression of their own personal opinions.

Vital 1 Students' Book

Ecoutez et répétez seulement le noms des animaux que vous aimez.

Copying

Categorisation can also easily be applied to copying tasks, to ensure that students concentrate on meaning rather than copying blindly. Students who enjoy copying should still be happy, and for those who don't, this does not feel too much like copying!

Ecris les loisirs en salle dans le cercle A.
Ecris les loisirs en plein air dans le cercle B.
Ecris les loisirs possibles en salle ou en plein air au centre.

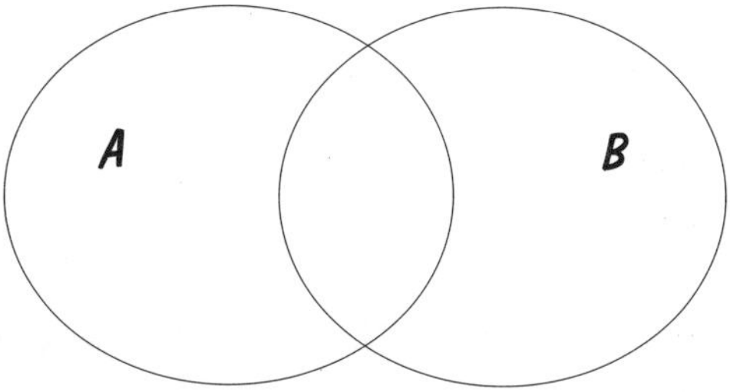

Personal opinions can also play a part in copying tasks.

Copie les phrases par ordre de préférence.
Devine l'ordre de ton/ta partenaire.
Comparez.

What has it got to do with me? – the real world dimension

Some students lose motivation after the 'fun and games' of the early stages because they cannot relate the foreign language to anything real. Two remedies need to be considered:

- setting the language whenever possible in its original context
- relating it to the students' own knowledge and experience.

Suggestions

Create a visual environment (posters, realia) which reflects more than just a holiday context.

Display simple news notices to be changed at regular intervals:

> Le sprinter britannique Linford Christie, champion olympique du 100 m, annonce qu'il va participer aux Jeux Olympiques d'Atlanta sur 100 m, 200 m et dans le relai 4 x 100 m.

Draw on students' extra-curricular knowledge. For instance, when doing work on recognising question patterns:

> ¿Dónde vive Batman?
> ¿Es periodista el señor Venables?
> ¿Cómo se llaman los hermanos del grupo Oasis?

Present language – especially revision of key stage 3 topics – in a vocational context that students of 14–16 can relate to.

1 Ecoutez et notez les numéros de téléphone.

2 Ecoutez les dialogues et notez qui a téléphoné. Ecrivez les noms.

3 Ecoutez. Il faut rappeler à quelle heure? Notez l'heure.

Vital 1 Students' Book

In the three tasks above, numbers, the alphabet and the time are being revised, but in a more mature, world-of-work context.

It's too easy! It's too hard! – differentiation

Students need to be presented with challenges suited to their needs, yet there can be a wide range of ability levels even among students preparing for the same examination tier. Setting different work for different students is not always the answer. Other methods may be more readily accepted by students while minimising preparation work and easing classroom management.

Suggestions

Making material go further

Set a series of increasingly difficult challenges all based on the same stimulus material. Using the materials below, students can be asked to:

- have a conversation with a partner
- have as many different conversations as they can in five minutes
- reuse the proposed structures to make up different answers, for instance 'J'ai passé mes vacances en Irlande'
- have a conversation without looking at the suggested answers
- block off the suggested answers and have a conversation, this time asking the questions in a different order
- write out a conversation
- learn a conversation by heart.

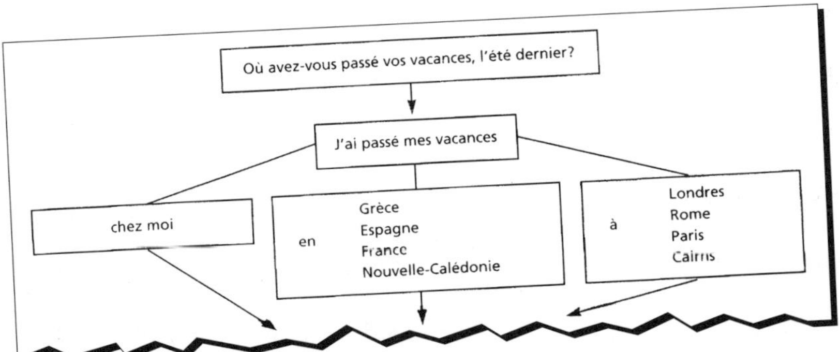

Vital 1 Students' Book

Present all the steps described above from the start. Students work more readily when they know in advance what they will be doing next.

Ask students to keep records of what they have done, both for your information and as motivation for them – students often tend to do more this way.

Depending on the activities and the students, you might like to set a minimum number of steps to be carried out, or to label each step as compulsory or optional.

Listening without tears

Set a differentiated series of expected outcomes all based on the same listening passage. Using different passages can cause problems.

Set a global aim which students can reach even though they might not grasp every single piece of information they hear.

> **Escucha los pasatiempos de las chicas: ¿cuál es la más/menos deportiva?**

Support

Vary the amount of support to be provided by setting limits on the use of reference materials: glossary, dictionary, list of key phrases, etc.

When setting work based on a model, set tasks where the model can be used in a variety of ways.

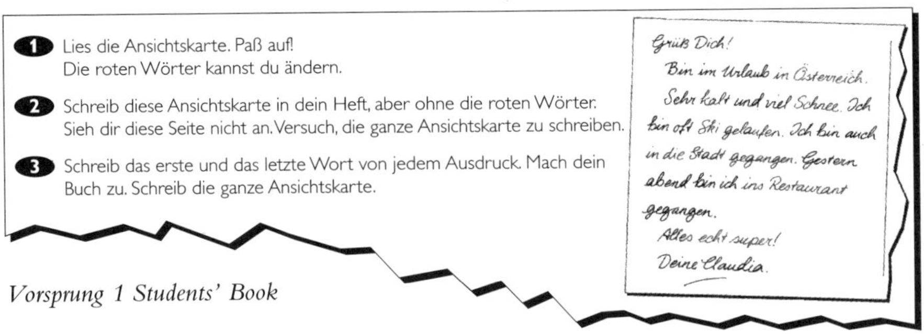

1. Lies die Ansichtskarte. Paß auf! Die roten Wörter kannst du ändern.
2. Schreib diese Ansichtskarte in dein Heft, aber ohne die roten Wörter. Sieh dir diese Seite nicht an. Versuch, die ganze Ansichtskarte zu schreiben.
3. Schreib das erste und das letzte Wort von jedem Ausdruck. Mach dein Buch zu. Schreib die ganze Ansichtskarte.

Grüß Dich!
Bin im Urlaub in Österreich. Sehr kalt und viel Schnee. Ich bin oft Ski gelaufen. Ich bin auch in die Stadt gegangen. Gestern abend bin ich ins Restaurant gegangen.
Alles echt super!
Deine Claudia.

Vorsprung 1 Students' Book

Alternatively, a task can first be practised using a model, then completed without one.

Speed

Ask students to time themselves when carrying out a task, giving them the opportunity to practise a few times first.

Extension – After they have practised a dialogue based on a model, faster/more able students can then create a more open-ended dialogue.

What did they say? – listening

Some students may find the absence of the written word in listening tasks rather frightening. For reassurance and therefore enhanced motivation and progress, students must learn to listen effectively.

Suggestions

Listening with a purpose

Train students to do detective work before any listening takes place. Students should use:

- the rubric
- the task itself (words and visuals)

to ascertain:

- what the passage is about
- what they have to listen out for.

After the detective work should come the warm-up. Encourage students to do some informed guessing based on the above by brainstorming on the relevant language, such as telling the time in Spanish and the words for getting up, breakfast, etc., for the task below.

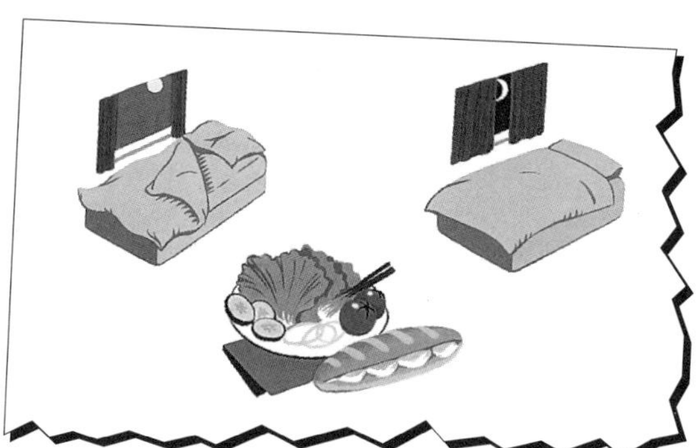

Tu amigo español habla de la rutina en su casa. Mira los dibujos y escribe a qué hora hacen cada cosa.

This is particularly useful at the revision stage, if a topic area has not been revisited for a while.

Take the brainstorming suggested above one step further by asking students to make blind guesses before they listen. For instance:

desayuno – ¿7.30?

This encourages students to listen more attentively to find out if any of their guesses were correct.

Avoid an excess of straight matching-up tasks. Use tasks where students have to draw conclusions, however simple. For instance, where the contents of several rooms are being described, but the names of the rooms are not mentioned, avoid providing pictures of the items, and make students write down the name of each room.

4 Hör zu. Welches Zimmer beschreibt man?

Vorsprung 1 Students' Book

Occasionally, for reassurance, signal when students are about to hear key language.

When listening to interviews, ask students not to write anything down the first time they listen. Instead, they should raise their hands whenever they recognise a question which signals that they are about to hear one of the answers they need.

Occasionally read out the tapescript so that the students can watch your lips. Do this instead of using the cassette or possibly after using the cassette, to give students an extra chance of completing their answers. Use intonation to emphasise some key language.

In the exam

- remind students to look at the examples provided. These might be easier to understand than the rubrics
- encourage students never to leave a blank
- explain that full sentences are not needed
- remind them they must answer in the correct language.

I can't say it properly! – speaking

'Speaking foreign' may not rate highly on the street credibility scale, and some students may be embarrassed. If that is the case, the emphasis on speaking has to be carefully disguised, for instance through games and competitions or training to beat the examiner at his/her own game.

Suggestions

For warming-up and revision at the beginning of a lesson, have a team activity challenging speed of response. Bring up a topic area (verbally or visually) and ask students to say words related to that topic. After one or two minutes, start asking for sentences.

Then move on to some selective repetition, again in teams if it helps.

When students practise structured dialogues based on a model, break the monotony by asking them to add one or more exchange of their choice to their dialogue. Compare the extra exchanges across the class and have a vote for the favourite ('favourite' goes down better than 'best').

Do not ask students to perform 'publicly' for the sake of it. Instead, have students help you put the others to the test. Ask the other students to listen to one of their classmates speaking and select pictures, words from a list, etc., as evidence that they understand what is being said. This method may also encourage peer correction and save you from having to interfere: if the students do not speak clearly enough, the others will soon intervene!

Here is another tip to encourage listening at the same time as speaking. After all the students have practised the same roleplay, ask each group to change one element of the roleplay script in secret. The whole class then listens to one or several groups and tries to spot the discrepancy. As an extra challenge, ask them to do this without referring back to their cue cards. This method can be used with any topic.

Vorsprung 1 Students' Book

A: Die Speisekarte, bitte.
B: Bitte sehr.
A: Einmal Melone, bitte, und einmal Krabbencocktail.
B: Ja, mein Herr, und nachher?
A: Zweimal Schweinekotelett, bitte.

To rekindle motivation and break the potential monotony of cue cards, provide pictures of famous people with little in common and ask students to make up a conversation between them on a given topic.

Topic – Qu'est-ce qu'on fait ce week-end?

Prince Charles: ____________________

Jon Bon Jovi: ____________________

PC: ____________________

JBJ: ____________________

Students should be reminded, however, to adhere as far as possible to language they have learnt. Again, get the class to vote for their favourite conversation.

General conversation

Vorsprung 1 Workbook

Exam Tip

Answer questions as fully as possible in your Speaking Exam. The more you can say, the more marks you will get.
If your examiner asks: *Hast du Geschwister?*, don't just say: *Ja, ich habe einen Bruder*, but carry on talking about your brother.
If you answer 'no' to a question, try to continue the sentence.

Example

Ich habe keine Haustiere, aber ich möchte einen Hund.

Practise this technique as a game by deliberately asking questions which would usually elicit a straightforward yes or no answer. Divide the class into two teams, each answering your questions in turn. Give points depending on quality of response. Penalise hesitancy. Ask one or two students to join you as the jury.

Also use the game approach to encourage longer responses. Set a minimum number of key points as a target.

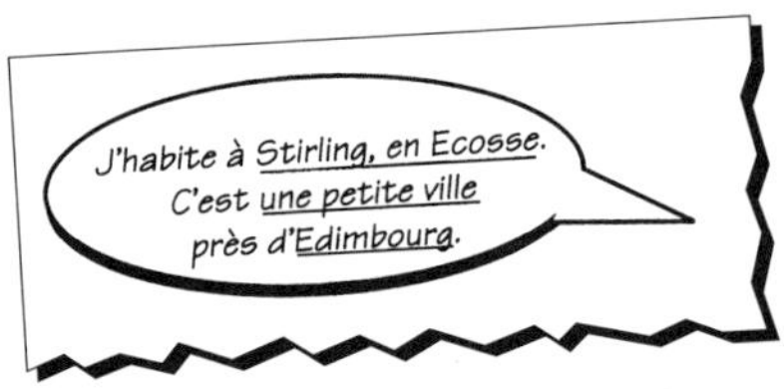

Vital 1 Workbook

In the exam

Students must:

- read the instructions carefully
- speak as clearly as possible
- hesitate as little as possible
- listen carefully to what the teacher says
- try to answer all the questions
- avoid just answering yes or no
- keep the conversation going
- think simple
- vary tenses
- give opinions as well as facts.

What does that word say? – reading

The written word is reassuring for some but can easily confuse others. Here again, lack of skill is often a greater problem than lack of knowledge. To sustain concentration, it is also important to vary the nature of the tasks.

Suggestions

Train students to study the rubrics first in order to narrow down their field of enquiry.

Ask students what methods they already know for understanding texts better, such as using visual support and cognates.

Remind students that they should start from what they *do* understand rather than be put off by what they do not.

Point out some other useful clues such as title, subheadings, layout or words in bold.

Numbers can be useful pointers. Ask students to spot all the numbers in a passage and say what they refer to.

Vital 1 Students' Book

Set a time limit for straight matching up tasks.

Liven up such tasks by including some superfluous items, then ask what would have been a suitable match for them.

Ask students to create their own matching up tasks, then swap with someone else.

For added interest, set a wider purpose than always fishing for detailed information.

A **1-Zi.-Appartement** (1-2 Personen)
GG, Wohnfläche ca. 40-56 qm, Wohn-Schlafraum mit Doppelschrankbett, Kochnische, Bad/WC, Terrasse.

B **3-Zi.-Appartement** (4-6 Personen)
im EG, Wohnfläche ca. 83-89 qm, Wohn-Schlafraum für 2 Personen, Doppelschlafzimmer, Einzelschlafraum (Etagenbett), Küche, Bad/WC, 1 Balkon.

Welches Appartement ist ideal für:

a eine Familie mit vier Kindern?
b ein junges Ehepaar?

Hilfe!
ein Ehepaar = ein Mann mit seiner Frau

Vorsprung 1 Students' Book

Add interest with a cross-curricular dimension.

Welche Länder sind Mitglieder der EU? Schreib diese Länder in dein Heft.

Österreich Italien Australien Spanien die USA Griechenland Irland

Vorsprung 1 Students' Book

Create a task within a task by providing the complete answers to one task, or several tasks, all mixed up. They have to sort them out.

As well as teaching the basics of dictionary use, treat dictionary avoidance techniques as a priority. Tell students why they should avoid using it (difficulty, pressure of time) and use these techniques regularly:

- do not always allow dictionary use
- set a maximum number of words to look up
- ask students to record how many words they have looked up
- ask them to complete all the answers they can before using the dictionary.

In the exam

As with listening tasks, students should look at the examples provided to understand the rubrics more easily. They should also:

- try to answer all questions; sensible guesses are better than a blank
- avoid writing their answers in full sentences
- use dictionaries only as a last resort, if there is time left
- answer in the correct language.

I can't spell! – writing

Although less confident students might prefer to do nothing but mindless copying, writing often remains the most despised skill. Even when students know the words to use, spelling gets in the way. And even holding a pen can demand considerable effort.

Suggestions

Explain that communication is rewarded (in some cases exclusively) in the exam in spite of inaccuracies. Make sure your marking reflects this.

Add a racing-against-the-clock element to simple tasks. Being the 'winner' may be more acceptable than 'getting a good mark'.

Schreib diese Listen ab. Was kannst du noch in jeder Liste schreiben? Wer kann die längsten Listen schreiben?

Warmes Essen	Kaltes Essen	Getränke
Currywurst	Käsebrot	Limo
Pommes Frites	Salamibrot	Cola

Vorsprung 1 Students' Book

To improve spelling, encourage students to set their own targets and build up their personal records.

J'ai bien écrit . . . mots nouveaux.
J'ai bien écrit . . . phrases nouvelles.

Charts can be used instead.

Provide opportunities for students to improve on their personal targets. Give them five minutes to learn before testing themselves. Then tell them that during the next lesson you will give them the opportunity to improve their score ('score' may go down better than 'mark').

Disguise writing by presenting it as a means to an end rather than an end in itself, for instance when asking students to make up tasks for others in the class:

- copying sentences and cutting them in half for matching up
- writing words for matching up with pictures
- changing sentences to make them false
- preparing a menu
- preparing a display.

Use IT:

- for its innate attraction
- to enable students to show off their IT skills
- for drafting and redrafting without a trace
- to motivate students with poor handwriting
- for experimenting with fonts, etc., for a top-class result.

In the exam

Students must:

- read the rubrics carefully
- do the correct number of tasks
- think simple
- strictly limit dictionary use
- underline useful structures and adapt them when a model is provided

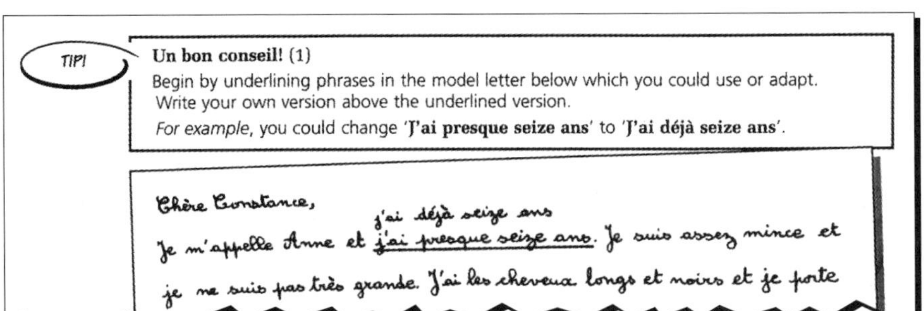
TIP!

Un bon conseil! (1)
Begin by underlining phrases in the model letter below which you could use or adapt.
Write your own version above the underlined version.
For example, you could change '**J'ai presque seize ans**' to '**J'ai déjà seize ans**'.

Chère Constance,
j'ai déjà seize ans
Je m'appelle Anne et j'ai presque seize ans. Je suis assez mince et
je ne suis pas très grande. J'ai les cheveux longs et noirs et je porte

Vital 2 Workbook

- vary tenses if possible
- include opinions as well as facts.

It's boring! – pace and variety

Working on oral skills for too long may be asking for chaos. Writing for too long may put students to sleep. On an educational level, progress in one skill reinforces progress in another. Balance is therefore essential.

Suggestions

Ensure a balance of skills in every lesson.

The variety of skills involved in language learning may lead students to feel they are continually jumping around from one skill to another. To break away from the patchiness students may feel, combine several skills within one task whenever possible. Explain each step clearly.

If mixed-skill tasks are too daunting, opt for a succession of tasks which are separate but related. For instance, as in the task below, use a listening task for checking the answers to a reading task.

1 Sieh dir diese Bilder an. Schreib einen Satz für jedes Bild.

2 Hör zu. Hattest du recht?

Vorsprung 1 Students' Book

Occasionally give a choice of outcome, oral or written.

1 Regardez ces renseignements.
Votre client(e) anglais(e) veut faire une excursion.

a Vous lui recommandez quelle excursion?
b Décrivez l'excursion.

2 Votre client(e) voudrait une description d'autres excursions. Vous pouvez décrire les trois autres excursions? Quelles sont les conditions?

Vital 1 Students' Book

Why can't you say it in English? – target language

What is more natural for a teacher than to use the foreign language as much as possible, since this is what you are supposed to teach? Yet does it make sense if students can't cope? But what will people think if they hear you use English? The simplest answer may be to use common sense as a guideline.

Suggestions

Always set yourself the target of maximum (but not necessarily exclusive) use of the foreign language. When a teacher joins a new school, departmental policy should help as regards the level of classroom interaction in the target language that students should be able to use or to understand, for instance.

When using the foreign language, use a variety of techniques to aid comprehension.

- give clear examples of what you want
- use cognates wherever possible
- use mime and facial expression to support meaning
- use visuals, if appropriate

Vital 1 Teachers' Resource Book

Always check that students have understood.

- use another student to demonstrate the activity
- use a reliable volunteer as an interpreter
- never let students start an activity if the instructions have not been clearly understood. It is better to resort to English than to have a confused class.

Vital 1 Teachers' Resource Book

Be realistic in your aims as regards students' use of the foreign language:

- have short total immersion time slots when only the target language is spoken (if you think this is all that can be achieved)
- be clear about the beginning and end of such slots
- reward effort, for instance through a tick system
- encourage students to help each other.

Do not be afraid to use English where necessary. This might mean giving a straight translation or explaining a structure, or could be for discipline purposes, positively as well as negatively. Chatting with students in English for two minutes at the beginning and the end of a lesson may do wonders in terms of establishing and sustaining a relationship with a difficult class.

I can't learn all that! – learning skills

Learning by heart is seen neither as fashionable nor enjoyable, yet it plays a significant part in language learning. Things become more complicated still when it comes to learning whole phrases or a paragraph rather than just words. The answer often consists of dressing up the learning by heart so as to make it more palatable.

Suggestions

As suggested under 'What does it mean anyway?'(p8–9), devote sufficient time to recognition, repetition and copying so as to set the memorisation process well on its way.

Brainstorm students on learning techniques and allow them to use the methods which work best for them: learning on their own from a bilingual list, learning with a friend, copying words etc.

Get students to set themselves targets and test each other.

Give them a time limit in which to memorise new items on the board or the overhead projector.

Disguise memorisation work under guessing tasks. Use whole-class approaches which students can then easily transfer into pair or group activities.

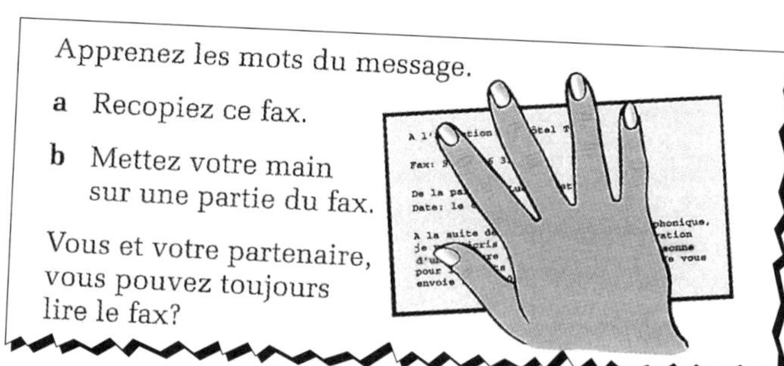

Vital 1
Students' Book

As a variation on the same idea, place one or several rulers across a page. For fun, use a comb instead: students are guaranteed to be glued to the screen trying to read between the teeth!

What's the point anyway? – revision and examination skills

Students sometimes give up before sitting the exam. Could this be because most do not know how to revise? Or because they are daunted by the enormity of the task? In addition, some students are convinced that teachers were born to make their lives miserable. Prove them wrong by showing them you are on their side: unravel all the exam mysteries for them.

Suggestions

Make sure students have a copy of the exam topics.

Be realistic. Do not necessarily expect students to revise much on their own. Integrate revision throughout the exam preparation years, then build it up nearer to the exam.

Teach revision skills.

- Copy the German phrases in a different order. Close your book. Write the English for each German phrase.
- Cover the German phrases which you copied. Look at the English phrases you wrote and write the German for each English phrase.
- Copy the title from one of the *Lernziele*. Count how many phrases there are in *Vorsprung* for that *Lernziel*. Try to write this number of phrases from memory.
- Copy the first and last words only from each key phrase. Close your book. Try to write the full phrase from memory.
- Create 'word suns'. Write a key word or phrase in the centre of your 'sun'. Write from memory as many associated words as possible.

Vorsprung 1 Workbook

Provide opportunities for practising those skills in class.

Rather than revision through looking or plain copying, suggest more attractive methods such as spiders' webs.

Revision should involve doing, not just relearning. To keep boredom at bay, find new contexts for revising 'old' language. For instance, if students have had enough of practising directions through town plans, try this exercise.

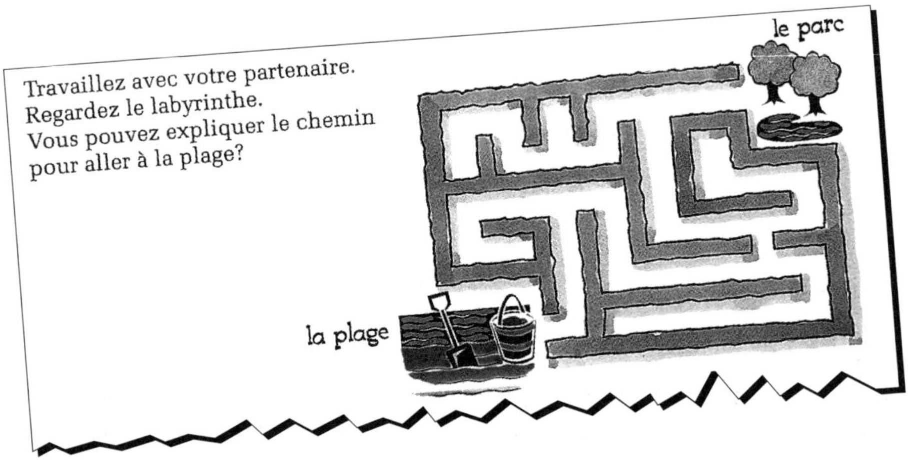

Vital 1 Students' Book

Use revision to enhance awareness that knowledge is transferable across topic areas, for instance by using key structures such as those below in different situations:

Be open about what can get students the grades on the day. Quote directly from examiners' reports if necessary.

Make sure students are clear about the format of each paper. Remind students about the potential pitfalls (excessive dictionary use, trying to write something too complicated etc.)

When using past papers in class, do not neglect quality for the sake of quantity. Ask students to do a few tasks rather than a whole paper, then devote plenty of time to constructive corrections.

Keep smiling and wish your students good luck!

Collins Tips for Busy Language Teachers

Motivating Reluctant Learners at 14–16

If you would like to inspect any of the other titles in this series or other resources mentioned in this book, please **tick the relevant boxes, fill in your details overleaf, photocopy or cut out this form and return** to:

HarperCollins Publishers
Modern Languages/Collins Educational
FREEPOST
London W6 8BR

Title	ISBN	Price	Approval/ Inspection Copy	Order Qty
Mixed Pack (1 copy of each)	0 00 320239 9	£11.70	☐	______
Stretching the More Able at 14-16	0 00 320227 5	£2.25		______
Brightening up Transactional Topics at 14-16	0 00 320228 3	£2.25		______
Independent Reading: how to make it work	0 00 320229 1	£2.25		______
Effective Use of a Bilingual Dictionary at 11–16	0 00 320230 5	£2.25		______
Homework and Cover Lessons: handy tips	0 00 320231 3	£2.25		______
Vorsprung 1 Students' Book	0 00 320135 X	£6.99	☐	______
Vorsprung 1 Teachers' Resource Book	0 00 320140 6	£11.50	☐	______
Vorsprung 1 Workbook	0 00 320136 8	£2.75	☐	______
Vital 1 Students' Book	0 00 320123 6	£6.99	☐	______
Vital 1 Teachers' Resource Book	0 00 320133 3	£9.50	☐	______
Vital 1 Workbook	0 00 320124 4	£2.50	☐	______
Vital 2 Students' Book	0 00 320128 7	£6.99	☐	______
Vital 2 Teachers' Resource Book	0 00 320134 1	£11.50	☐	______
Vital 2 Workbook	0 00 320157 0	£2.50	☐	______
Modern Languages Catalogue	0 58 380108 0	FREE		______

We are always looking to expand the *Collins Tips for Busy Language Teachers* series and would be interested to know what topics you would like to see covered in the future. (Please tick the boxes below or add your own suggestions.)

☐ Post-16: bridging the gap

☐ Making Grammar Practice at 14–16 More Fun

☐ Languages for Special Needs Students at 14–16

☐ Testing in the Target Language

☐ Other ______________________________

Mr/Ms/Miss/Mrs: ______________________________

Position: ______________________________

School: ______________________________

Address: ______________________________

____

____

Postcode: ______________________________

LEA: ______________________________

E-mail address: ______________________________

Code:1491